CAST IRON COOKBOOK

*Delicious Recipes and Tips for Cooking
with Cast Iron Skillets and Dutch Ovens
(2023 Guide for Beginners)*

Ursa Craig

Table of Contents

Introduction

This book was written to show you a more modern way to use cast iron in your everyday cooking. While cast iron has a reputation for rustic camping cooking, we would be doing it a disservice if we overlooked the sophistication and simplicity that it can bring to your kitchen on a daily basis. If you've been looking for a way to simplify meal preparation without sacrificing any culinary elements, then adopting the cast iron lifestyle will bring you a lot of joy in the kitchen.

Each recipe in this book was designed to maximize flavor while minimizing effort. Entire meals can be prepared in a single skillet that can be used on the stovetop, in the oven, or both. Your entire meal is contained in one skillet that has enhanced both the flavor and character of your favorite dishes, from hearty stews to delicate seafood pasta.

There are a few things you should know about cast iron cooking, which we will go over shortly. However, there are a few tricks that will make your one-skillet cooking even easier, as well as reduce the amount of time you spend in the kitchen.

First, familiarize yourself with your recipe and gather all of your ingredients. Because cast iron retains heat so well, you may notice that your food cooks a little faster than usual. Whereas you may have previously had time to leisurely chop ingredients while cooking, you may find that when using cast iron, it is better to have everything prepared ahead of time.

Take advantage of the pre-preparation of ingredients. An easy cast iron skillet dinner can be made with a variety of fresh produce and meats, as well as pre-cooked pasta or grains, the majority of which can be conveniently stored in your freezer until ready to use. When it comes to pasta, the noodles can often be cooked directly in the skillet with a few cups of broth or water. It is also a good idea to have some precooked noodles on hand, lightly dressed in olive oil to prevent sticking. These are ideal for dishes with cream sauces.

Experiment frequently. Take note of the preparation techniques and general style of foods presented as you begin to make the recipes in this book, and then experiment on your own. The more you do it, the more at ease you will be with using cast iron.

You do not require the entire cast iron set. Don't feel obligated to purchase an entire set of cookware that you believe you will never use. Instead, use a single large skillet. All of the recipes in this book are made in a 10-inch or 12-inch skillet. Many of these recipes can be scaled down and cooked in smaller skillets, but if you only have one piece of cast iron, a larger skillet will provide more versatility.

Cast Iron Skillet Maintenance and Use

Caring for and using your cast iron skillet necessitate only a few special considerations, but this does not imply that it is more difficult or difficult to use than any other type of cookware. The following tips will help you get the most out of your cast iron cookware.

Seasoning

To begin, your cast iron needs a good seasoning, and we don't mean spice. Seasoning your cast iron skillet entails applying thin layers of oil and repeatedly heating it. This converts the cooking oil into a type of polymerized oil. Simply put, seasoning your pan forms a barrier between your food and the pan, making it nonstick, increasing its lifespan, and decreasing the possibility of the metal reacting with more acidic ingredients. Your pan will need to be seasoned when you first buy it, and then on a regular basis thereafter. Seasoning your cast iron skillet can be done in two ways:

Method No. 1

Begin by washing your cast iron gently with mild soap. This should be a quick wash; do not immerse your cast iron in the water. Preheat the oven to 350°F/177°C and thoroughly dry your skillet.

Turn on a low burner and gently heat the pan. Remove the pan from the heat and coat it with vegetable oil (corn oil works well). Ensure that the entire surface is covered, but leave no excess to drip or puddle.

Place the pan in the oven and leave it for about an hour. Allow cooling before using.

Method No. 2

Pour a layer of coarse salt thick enough to cover the entire bottom of your cast iron skillet without allowing you to see through it. Pour in just enough cooking oil to cover the salt.

Heat the oil over medium heat until it starts to smoke.

(If necessary, raise the temperature.)

Pour the salt and oil mixture into a heat-resistant container and set aside.

Buff the inside of the pan with a clean, soft cloth until it is smooth.

Cleaning

While some may argue that cast iron does not need to be cleaned after each use, the truth is that it does, albeit in a different way than you may be accustomed to. Contrary to popular belief, water is not the enemy of cast iron, especially seasoned cast iron. After each use, thoroughly rinse and dry your pan, only using a very mild soap if necessary. The drying process is critical here. If you leave any moisture in the pan before storing it, it will rust. You may occasionally have food caked onto your skillet that is difficult to remove. Avoid using abrasive scouring materials, which will damage the oil coating of your seasoning and, eventually, the pan itself. Instead, use a salt and fat method similar to the one described above, but in smaller quantities and at a lower heat. Gently loosen stuck food with a cloth, using the salt as an abrasive and the fat as a lubricant.

Re-seasoning

Make sure to thoroughly dry the skillet after each use. Place a freshly rinsed skillet on a burner over high heat to help evaporate any moisture left behind. Rub a small amount of cooking oil over the surface with a paper towel and heat until it smokes. Remove from the heat and set aside to cool. Your seasoning layer will be built up over time to the point where this only needs to be done on occasion.

Cooking Preparation

Cast iron is great because it efficiently retains heat — it gets hot and stays hot. However, because cast iron has a lower thermal conductivity, it is more prone to hot spots, or areas where food cooks faster than others. You may find this useful for some dishes; however, to minimize this effect, you should prepare your skillet by placing it dry over a heat source for several minutes before you begin cooking. To help spread the heat evenly throughout the pan, rotate the skillet every 30 seconds or so.

Acidity

The metal in your cast iron skillet may react with certain acidic foods, altering the flavor and deteriorating the skillet. It is not necessary to avoid acidic foods entirely; however, when working with acidic foods, it is critical to keep your pan properly seasoned and to limit the time acidic foods are in the pan whenever possible. Tomatoes and tomato sauces, for example, are added to dishes without issue. It is not recommended, however, to make a tomato sauce from scratch in a cast iron pan, which requires hours of simmering. Deglazing with wine is delicious and acceptable as long as the process is limited to a few minutes.

Sweet and savory

Cast iron tends to retain some flavors. As a result, if you intend to do a lot of cast iron cooking, buy at least two separate pieces: one for sweet dishes and one for savory dishes. This will keep the hint of seared steak with mushrooms out of your apple crisp!

That's it for the fundamentals of cast iron cooking. It's not at all intimidating. All that remains is for you to tackle and enjoy the recipes that follow.

Recipes for Chicken

Chicken Parmesan from the Old World

4 people
Time to prepare: 10 minutes
Time to cook: 30 minutes

14 cups olive oil 4 boneless, skinless chicken breasts, pounded thin
14 cup shallots, sliced 2 teaspoons fresh rosemary, chopped 14 cups fresh basil, chopped 2 teaspoons fresh thyme, chopped 14 cups fresh parsley, chopped 1 teaspoon salt teaspoon black pepper
14 cups red wine, dry
12 cup tomato sauce or marinara
12lb dry vermicelli noodles
1 cup shredded fresh mozzarella cheese 12 cup freshly grated parmesan cheese

Preheat oven to 450°F/432°C before beginning.

Warm the olive oil in a 12-inch cast iron skillet over medium heat.

Cook until the chicken is lightly browned on both sides, about 2-3 minutes per side.

Stir in the garlic and shallots. Season the chicken with salt, black pepper, rosemary, basil, thyme, and parsley. Allow the red wine to reduce for 1-2 minutes.

Stir in the tomato or marinara sauce and spoon it over the chicken. Split the vermicelli noodles in half and distribute them throughout the sauce. Simmer for 3 minutes before removing from the heat.

Top the chicken with mozzarella cheese first, then parmesan cheese.

Place in the oven for 20 minutes, or until the cheese is bubbly and golden.

Allow cooling for a few minutes before serving.

Skillet Creamy Chicken Enchilada

4-6 people
Time to prepare: 10 minutes
Time to cook: 20 minutes

1 pound boneless, skinless chicken breast (cubed)
1 tablespoon extra virgin olive oil
3 crushed and minced garlic cloves
1 tsp. chili powder
12 tablespoons cumin
1 teaspoon sea salt
1 teaspoon black pepper cup sliced white mushrooms
cup shredded spinach
1 pound black beans (canned or precooked)
12 cups cooked rice, divided cups salsa verde or green
enchilada sauce

12 cups soured cream
14 cups softened cream cheese
6-8 corn or flour tortillas
12 c. Monterey Jack cheese
12 cup queso Mexicano
Garnish with fresh cilantro

Preheat the broiler to high.
Warm the olive oil in a 12-inch cast iron skillet over medium heat.
Cook, stirring occasionally until the chicken is browned, about 5 minutes.
Season with chili powder, cumin, salt, and black pepper to taste. To combine, stir everything together.
Sauté for 2-3 minutes with the mushrooms and spinach before adding the black beans and rice. Stir thoroughly.
Combine 1 cup of the salsa verde, sour cream, and cream cheese in a mixing bowl. Add to the skillet and stir until creamy.
Cover the contents of the skillet with flour or corn tortillas, one or two layers thick.
Top with the remaining salsa verde, then the Monterey jack cheese and the Mexican queso cheese.
Cook for 5-10 minutes, or until the cheese is melted and lightly browned, under the broiler.
Before serving, garnish with fresh cilantro.

Baked Basil Balsamic Chicken

4 people
Time to prepare: 5 minutes
Time to cook: 30 minutes

1 12-pound boneless and skinless chicken breast
1 tablespoon olive oil 1 cup sliced red onion halved
cups sugar snap peas, small red potatoes, washed and
trimmed cloves crushed and minced garlic
14 cups heavy cream 1 cup chicken stock 14 cup
balsamic vinegar 1 teaspoon honey
1 fresh rosemary sprig
14 cups chopped fresh basil 1 teaspoon sea salt
1 teaspoon ground black pepper

Preheat the oven to 400 degrees Fahrenheit/204 degrees
Celsius.
Warm the olive oil in a 12-inch cast iron skillet over
medium heat.
Brown the chicken on both sides for about 3-5 minutes
per side. Set aside after removing from the pan.
Combine the red potatoes, sugar snap peas, and garlic in
a mixing bowl. Cook for 5 minutes, or until the potatoes
start to brown. If necessary, add more olive oil. Remove
the chicken from the pan and set aside.
Reduce the balsamic vinegar in the pan for 1-2 minutes,
scraping the skillet as you go.

Constantly stir in the chicken stock, heavy cream, and honey. Season with rosemary, basil, salt, and pepper to taste.

Return the chicken to the skillet, then add the vegetables.

Bake the skillet for 20 minutes, or until the chicken is cooked through and the juices run clear.

Roasted Sage Chicken with Rustic Vegetables

4 people
Time to prepare: 10 minutes
Time to cook: 50 minutes

Ingredients:

4 chicken breasts, bone-in 12 cups extra virgin olive oil

2 cups halved red potatoes

2 cups mini portabella mushrooms, whole

1 cup red onion, thickly sliced

4 crushed and minced garlic cloves

12 cup chicken broth

1 teaspoon of lemon juice

1 tablespoon sage leaves, whole

1 tsp salt, 1 tsp ground black peppercorns

1 sliced lemon

Preheat the oven to 400 degrees Fahrenheit/204 degrees Celsius.

Warm the olive oil in a 12-inch cast iron skillet over medium heat.

Cook the chicken for 3 minutes on one side. Stir in the red potatoes, portabella mushrooms, red onion, and garlic. Cook for another 5-7 minutes, or until the chicken is browned on the outside.

Combine the chicken stock, lemon juice, whole sage, salt, and ground peppercorns in a mixing bowl. Toss gently to combine. Arrange the lemon slices on top of the chicken and vegetables.

Bake for 40 minutes, or until the chicken is cooked through and the juices run clear.

Sundried Tomato Spinach Stuffed Chicken

4 people
Time to prepare: 15 minutes
Time to cook: 40 minutes

4 boneless, skinless chicken breasts, split down the
middle
12 cup bacon, diced 2 garlic cloves, crushed and minced
2 cups spinach, chopped 12 cups jarred sundried
tomatoes, chopped
12 cups freshly grated parmesan cheese 14 cups
chopped fresh parsley 2 eggs, beaten
1 teaspoon sea salt
1 teaspoon ground black pepper
1 cup chopped red onion 4 cups cubed sweet potato 14
teaspoon nutmeg
14 teaspoons dried oregano
12 tsp. paprika
1 tablespoon extra virgin olive oil
1 cup chicken broth
1 cup shredded smoked provolone cheese

Preheat the oven to 375°F (191°C).
Heat the bacon in a 12-inch cast iron skillet over
medium heat. Cook until the bacon is semi-crisp, about
5 minutes.

Sauté for 1 minute with the garlic before adding the spinach and sundried tomatoes. Sauté for 2-3 minutes, stirring gently.

Transfer the mixture to a bowl with a slotted spoon and set aside to cool slightly.

Cook, stirring occasionally, for 5 minutes with the sweet potatoes and onion in the skillet. Nutmeg, oregano, and paprika to taste. Cook for 3 minutes more before removing from the pan. Keep the heat on medium and add the olive oil to the pan.

Combine the seasoned bread crumbs, parmesan cheese, fresh parsley, salt, and black pepper in a mixing bowl.

Fill each chicken breast halfway with the spinach mixture. Brush each piece of chicken with the beaten egg before dredging in the breadcrumb mixture.

Cook the chicken in the pan for 3-4 minutes, or until lightly browned on each side.

Return the sweet potatoes to the pan and pour in the chicken stock. Shredded provolone cheese should be used to cover the chicken.

Bake the skillet for 20-25 minutes, or until the chicken is cooked through and the juices run clear.

Ranch Rice with Buffalo Chicken

4 people
Time to prepare: 10 minutes
Time to cook: 30 minutes

4 chicken breasts, boneless and skinless
12 cups diced bacon, 1 cup red onion, 1 cup celery, 1
cup carrots, 4 cups cooked rice
2 cup chicken broth
14 cups fresh parsley, chopped 2 teaspoons fresh dill
1 tsp. onion powder
1 teaspoon black pepper 1 teaspoon salt
14–12 cup buffalo sauce, depending on taste

12 cups crumbled blue cheese

Preheat the oven to 400 degrees Fahrenheit/204 degrees Celsius.
Heat the bacon in a 12-inch cast iron skillet over medium heat. Cook for 5 minutes, or until browned.
Combine the red onion, celery, and carrots in a mixing bowl. Cook for 5 minutes, then remove with a slotted spoon. Place aside.
Brown the chicken in the skillet for 3-5 minutes on each side. Return the sautéed vegetables to the skillet with the rice and chicken stock. Combine thoroughly.
Dill, parsley, onion powder, salt, and black pepper to taste. Combine the buffalo sauce and blue cheese in a mixing bowl. Gently combine.
Bake for 20 minutes, or until the chicken is cooked through and the juices run clear.

Roasted Chicken with Dijon and Wine

4-6 people

Time to prepare: 15 minutes

1 hour of cooking

2 pounds bone-in, skin-on assorted chicken pieces

12 cups cubed pancetta 14 cups sliced shallots

2 cups halved Brussels sprouts 14 cup mustard Dijon

1 tbsp Herbes de Provence

1 teaspoon sea salt

1 teaspoon peppercorns, ground

12 cups all-purpose flour

1 cup chicken broth

12 cups white wine, dry

Preheat the oven to 350 degrees Fahrenheit/177 degrees Celsius.

Heat the pancetta in a 12-inch cast iron skillet over medium heat. Cook the pancetta for 5 minutes, or until crispy.

Cook for another 1-2 minutes, stirring frequently, before adding the Brussels sprouts and cooking for another 5 minutes, stirring frequently.

Remove the Brussels sprouts, shallots, and pancetta with a slotted spoon. Place aside.

In a mixing bowl, combine the flour, Herbs de Provence, salt, and ground peppercorns. Combine thoroughly.

Brush the chicken with Dijon mustard and then lightly dredge in the flour mixture.

Return the chicken to the skillet and brown it on both sides over medium heat with the remaining pancetta grease (adding more olive oil if necessary).

Reduce the white wine for 2 minutes, then add the chicken stock, Brussels sprouts, and pancetta to the skillet.

Bake for 35-40 minutes, or until the chicken is crispy brown and cooked through to an internal temperature of at least 165°F/74°C.

Before serving, transfer to serving plates and drizzle with pan sauce.

Peanut Noodles with Spicy Chicken and Lemongrass

4 people
Time to prepare: 10 minutes
Time to cook: 20 minutes

1 pound boneless skinless chicken breast, cubed
teaspoons olive oil 12 cup soy sauce crushed and
minced garlic cloves
1 tablespoon grated fresh ginger 1 tablespoon chopped
fresh lemongrass 1 tablespoon chili garlic paste
12 cups natural creamy peanut butter
1 tbsp lime juice
1 tbsp sesame oil
2 cups chicken broth
12 lb angel hair pasta
12 cups chopped peanuts Scallions, sliced for garnish

Preparation: Heat the olive oil in a 12-inch cast iron
skillet over medium heat.
Cook until the chicken is golden brown, about 5
minutes.
Combine the soy sauce, garlic, ginger, lemongrass, and
chili garlic paste in a mixing bowl. Cook for 1-2
minutes with the chicken.
Combine the peanut butter, lime juice, sesame oil, and
chicken stock in a mixing bowl. Increase the heat to
medium-high until the stock begins to boil. Reduce the
heat to low and add the angel hair pasta. Cook for about
5-7 minutes, or until the noodles are tender.
Remove from heat and sprinkle with peanuts before
serving.

Recipes for Beef

Cornbread with Mole Chile

6 people
Time to prepare: 15 minutes
Time to cook: 45 minutes

1 pound cooked ground beef
4 crushed and minced garlic cloves
2 cups dried black beans (canned or precooked)
1 cup dried kidney beans (canned or precooked)
15 oz. fire-roasted tomatoes cup fresh corn kernels
4 cups beef broth
two tbsp tomato paste
2 tbsp cocoa powder, unsweetened
14 tbsp smoked paprika
1 tsp. ancho chili powder
1 teaspoon ground cinnamon
1 teaspoon sea salt
1 teaspoon ground black pepper
1 cup cornmeal blend
1 beaten egg 14 cups vegetable oil
a quarter cup whole milk
1 cup shredded cheddar cheese
Scallions for decoration

Preheat the oven to 425°F/218°C before beginning.

Add the ground beef and garlic to a 12-inch deep cast iron skillet. Cook for 5-7 minutes, or until browned, over medium heat. Remove any remaining grease from the meat.

Combine the black beans, kidney beans, fire-roasted tomatoes, and corn in a mixing bowl. To combine, stir everything together.

Gently push the ingredients to the skillet's outer rim. Add the beef stock, tomato paste, cocoa powder, smoked paprika, ancho chili powder, and cinnamon to the center.

Stir the seasonings together in the center of the skillet, then begin to incorporate the rest of the ingredients, eventually mixing everything together throughout the skillet. Season to taste with salt and black pepper.

Reduce the heat to low and leave to simmer while you prepare the cornbread topping.

Combine the cornmeal mixture, egg, vegetable oil, whole milk, and cheddar cheese in a mixing bowl.

Spread the mixture over the chili, starting in the center and working your way out to the pan's edges.

Preheat the oven to 25-30 minutes, or until the top is golden brown.

Before serving, garnish with scallions.

Stuffed Pepper Casserole in Three Colors

4 people
Time to prepare: 10 minutes
Time to cook: 30 minutes

1 pound ground beef 4 tablespoons olive oil cloves
crushed and minced garlic
1 cup red bell pepper, diced 1 cup yellow bell pepper,
diced 1 cup green bell pepper, diced 12 cup red onion,
diced 14 cup fresh basil, chopped 14 cup parsley,
chopped
1 cup beef broth
1 tsp. Worcestershire sauce
1 cup raw rice 1 teaspoon salt
1 teaspoon ground black pepper
1 cup shredded provolone cheese 12 cups freshly grated
parmesan cheese

Preparation: Heat the olive oil in a 10- or 12-inch cast iron skillet over medium heat.
Cook the ground beef until it is browned, then drain any excess fat.
Combine the garlic, red bell pepper, yellow bell pepper, green bell pepper, and red onion in a mixing bowl.
Cook for 3-5 minutes.
Season with basil and parsley to taste. Combine the tomato sauce, beef stock, and Worcestershire sauce in a mixing bowl. Stir, then turn the heat up to medium-high and bring to a boil.
Combine the rice, salt, and black pepper in a mixing bowl. Reduce the heat to low and cover. Cook for about 15-20 minutes, or until the rice is tender.
Cover and cook for another 5 minutes, or until the cheese is melted, over the rice.

Pizza for Beef Lovers Deep Dish

4-6 people
Time to prepare: 15 minutes
Time to cook: 30 minutes

14 cups shallots, sliced 2 cups portabella mushrooms, sliced 1 pound flank steak, sliced into thin strips cloves garlic, crushed and minced
1 teaspoon red pepper flakes, crushed
1 teaspoon salt, 1 teaspoon black pepper, 1 tablespoon olive oil, divided 1 premade pizza dough ball, enough for one large pizza
12 cup smoked Gouda, cut into very small cubes 1 cup canned fire roasted tomatoes, drained 1 cup heirloom tomatoes, sliced
1 cup shredded fresh mozzarella 12 cup freshly grated parmesan

Preheat oven to 425°F/218°C before beginning.
1 tablespoon olive oil, heated in a 12-inch cast iron skillet over medium heat
Combine the steak strips, garlic, and shallots in a mixing bowl. Cook, stirring occasionally, for about 5 minutes, or until the steak is almost done. Sauté the mushrooms, red pepper flakes, salt, and black pepper for 2 minutes more.
Remove the contents with a slotted spoon and set aside. Allow the skillet to cool enough to handle.

Roll out the dough into a large circle with a diameter of at least 14 inches. Press the dough directly into the pan, on top of any remaining pan drippings. Spread the dough across the bottom and up the sides of the skillet. Brush the remaining olive oil over the dough and top with the heirloom tomatoes. Then add the beef and mushroom mixture, then the Gouda cheese.

Spread the fire-roasted tomatoes over the top as evenly as possible. Then sprinkle with mozzarella and parmesan cheese.

Cook for 3-5 minutes over medium heat before placing in the oven and baking for 15-20 minutes, or until the crust is golden brown and the cheese is bubbly.

Allow resting for a few minutes before serving.

Lasagna with a Rich Heritage

4 people

Time to prepare: 10 minutes
Time to cook: 30 minutes

1 tablespoon extra virgin olive oil
1 cup diced red onion 12 cups diced red bell pepper
4 crushed and minced garlic cloves
1 pound crumbled ground beef 12 cups fresh basil
chopped 1 tablespoon fresh oregano chopped 1
teaspoon salt
1 teaspoon ground black pepper
4 cup canned fire-roasted tomatoes, liquid
10 lasagna noodles, cut into 2-3 inch chunks
1 cup shredded fresh mozzarella cheese
1 pound of ricotta cheese
12 cups grated parmesan cheese

Preheat the oven to broil.
Warm the olive oil in a 12-inch cast iron skillet over
medium heat.
Cook until the ground beef is browned, about 7 minutes.
Remove any excess fat.
Combine the red onion, bell pepper, and garlic in a
mixing bowl. Cook, stirring constantly, until the onion
and pepper are slightly tender, about 3 minutes.
Season with basil, oregano, salt, and pepper to taste.
Increase the heat to medium-high and add the tomatoes.
Bring to a low boil, then stir in the lasagna noodles and
reduce to a simmer.

10 minutes in the oven

Combine the mozzarella, ricotta, and parmesan cheeses in a mixing bowl. Combine thoroughly.

Spoon the cheese mixture all over the skillet.

Broil the skillet for 5-7 minutes, or until the cheese is lightly browned.

Allow cooling for a few minutes before serving.

Tomatoes and Italian Beef

4 people
Time to prepare: 10 minutes
Time to cook: 25 minutes

2 pounds choice beef steak, approximately 112 inches
thick 14 cup olive oil, divided

5 garlic cloves, crushed and minced

4 cups halved mini tomatoes in various colors

3 cups shredded fresh spinach

1 fresh rosemary sprig

1 tablespoon thyme, fresh

12 cups chopped fresh basil

1 teaspoon coarse sea salt

1 teaspoon black peppercorns, ground

3 tbsp olive oil (divided)

Preheat the oven to 375°F (191°C).

Heat two tablespoons of olive oil in a 12-inch cast iron skillet over medium-high heat.

Cook for 1 minute after adding the garlic. Sauté the tomatoes for 2 minutes before adding the spinach. Cook for another 1-2 minutes, or until the spinach has wilted slightly. Set aside the contents with a slotted spoon.

Pour the remaining oil into the skillet. Add the steaks to the hot oil and season with salt and ground black peppercorns. Sear the steaks until brown on both sides, about 7 minutes per side.

Return the tomatoes and spinach to the pan. Season with rosemary, thyme, and basil to taste. Place the skillet in the oven and bake for 6-10 minutes, or until the steak is done to your liking.

Allow 10 minutes to rest before serving.

Flank Steak with Creamy Basil Sauce

4 people
Time to prepare: 10 minutes
Time to cook: 30 minutes

2 pounds flank steak, pounded to an even thickness
1 tbsp. vegetable oil
3 crushed and minced garlic cloves
1 tsp Worcestershire sauce
1 teaspoon sea salt
1 teaspoon ground black pepper
4 cups washed and trimmed green beans
12 cups beef broth tsp cornstarch tsp ground black
peppercorns

14 cups chopped fresh basil

12 teaspoon salt 1 tablespoon chopped chives

12 cups softened cream cheese

Preparation: Heat the vegetable oil in a 12-inch cast iron skillet over medium-high heat.

Season the steak with garlic, Worcestershire sauce, salt, and black pepper in the pan. Sear until browned on both sides, about 10 minutes per side. Remove the steak from the pan and place it on a plate to rest.

Meanwhile, add the green beans to the pan and sauté in the meat juices for 3-4 minutes, or until the color brightens. Remove the steak and set it aside.

Combine the beef broth and cornstarch in a small bowl. Whisk until smooth, then pour into the hot skillet.

Season with salt, black peppercorns, basil, and chives. Combine thoroughly.

Whisk in the cream cheese until it has broken up and blended smoothly with the broth in the pan. 12 minutes in the oven

Serve the warm basil sauce alongside the steak and green beans.

Dumplings with Beef and Rosemary

6 people
Time to prepare: 15 minutes
Time to cook: 35 minutes

2 pounds of beef stew meat 14 cup flour 1 teaspoon
paprika
1 tsp. garlic powder
1 tablespoon butter 1 teaspoon black pepper 1 teaspoon
thyme
2 crushed and minced garlic cloves
1 cup chopped red onion 12 cups diced celery 2 cups
beef broth
1-quart apple cider
1 cup chopped carrots

1 cup fresh peas 1 cup chopped parsnips 14 cup flour 14
cup seasoned bread crumbs tablespoons vegetable
shortening
1 tablespoon chopped fresh rosemary
12 teaspoon salt 1 teaspoon fresh dill
12 tsp black pepper
1 beaten egg

14 cup flour, paprika, garlic powder, black pepper, and
thyme in a mixing bowl Coat the stew meat pieces in
the seasoned flour. Place aside.
Heat the butter in a 12-inch cast iron skillet over
medium heat. Combine the garlic, red onion, and celery
in a mixing bowl. Cook for 23 minutes.
Cook for 5 minutes, or until the beef is browned.
Scrape the pan and add the beef stock and apple cider.
Bring the water to a boil over medium-high heat.
Reduce the heat to medium-low and stir in the carrots,
peas, and parsnips. Cover and leave to cook for 45
minutes.
In the meantime, whisk together 14 cup flour, bread
crumbs, vegetable shortening, rosemary, dill, salt, black
pepper, and egg. Mix everything together until a dough
forms. Form the dough into rough ball-shaped
dumplings with tablespoon-sized mounds.
Cook the dumplings in the stew for another 15 minutes
before serving.

Jasmine rice and Korean spiced beef

4 people
Time to prepare: 10 minutes
Time to cook: 20 minutes

2 tablespoons vegetable oil 1 pound beef steak cut into
thin strips
14 cups soy sauce tbsp brown sugar
1 tbsp. honey 1 tbsp. sesame seeds 1 tsp. sesame oil
2 tbsp. garlic paste
2 crushed and minced garlic cloves
1 cup yellow onion, 1 cup sliced savoy cabbage, 1 cup
shredded broccoli florets
1 cup carrots, thinly sliced
Scallions, sliced for garnish, 4 cups jasmine rice

Preparation: Heat the vegetable oil in a 10- or 12-inch
cast iron skillet over medium-high heat. Sauté the steak
for 2-3 minutes, or until browned. Move the meat to the
skillet's outer edges.
Add the soy sauce, brown sugar, honey, sesame seeds,
sesame oil, and garlic paste to the center of the skillet.
Stir for 1 minute, or until fragrant.
Mix in the garlic and onion. Cook for 2 minutes.
Savoy cabbage, broccoli, and carrots should be added
now. Cook for 3 minutes before returning the meat to
the center of the pan.
Just before serving, add the jasmine rice.

Garnish with scallions, if desired.

Hamburger Casserole with Everything

4 people

Time to prepare: 10 minutes
Time to cook: 20 minutes

1 pound ground beef cup red onion, diced cups tomatoes, diced

14 cup ketchup 14 cup mustard

14 teaspoons Worcestershire sauce

14 cups diced dill pickles

1 tbsp. vegetable oil

4 cups shredded potatoes (moistened)

1 tsp. garlic powder

1 teaspoon dried oregano

1 teaspoon sea salt

1 teaspoon ground black pepper

1 cup shredded cheddar cheese

Preparation: Heat a 12-inch skillet over medium heat with the ground beef. Cook for 4-5 minutes, or until lightly browned. Remove any excess fat.
Combine the red onion and tomatoes in a mixing bowl. 3-4 minutes in the oven Season with ketchup, mustard, Worcestershire sauce, and dill pickles to taste. Combine thoroughly. Set aside after removing from the skillet. Increase the heat to medium-high and add the vegetable oil to the pan. Mix in the shredded potatoes. Cook for 3 minutes while tossing. Garlic powder, oregano, salt, and black pepper to taste. Cook for 5 minutes, or until the

bottom becomes crispy, after pressing the potatoes into the pan.

Return the ground beef to the skillet and toss it with the potatoes. Cook for another 3-5 minutes, or until thoroughly heated.

Before serving, sprinkle with shredded cheddar cheese.

Recipes for Pork

Creamy Mac and Cheese with Pancetta and Scallions

4-6 people

Time to prepare: 15 minutes
Time to cook: 40 minutes

1 pound elbow macaroni, cooked 12 pound pancetta,
cubed garlic cloves, crushed and minced 12 cup
scallions, sliced 14 cup butter
14 cup flour 12 cup milk or heavy cream
2 cups shredded Swiss cheese 2 cups shredded white
cheddar cheese 12 cup freshly grated parmesan cheese
1 tsp nutmeg, 1 tsp paprika, 1 tsp Dijon mustard
12 cup bread crumbs, seasoned

Preheat the oven to 400 degrees Fahrenheit/204 degrees
Celsius.
Heat the pancetta in a 12-inch cast iron skillet over
medium-high heat. Cook until crispy, about 5 minutes.
Stir in the garlic and scallions. 2 minutes in the oven Set
aside and remove with a slotted spoon.
Turn the heat down to medium. Cook until the butter is
melted. Mix in the flour until a thick, lightly browned
paste forms.
Whisk in the milk or heavy cream slowly. Bring to a
boil while constantly stirring. Reduce the heat to low
and allow it to simmer.
Combine the Swiss, cheddar, parmesan, nutmeg,
paprika, and Dijon mustard in a mixing bowl. Stir
thoroughly.

Return the cooked macaroni noodles and pancetta to the pan. Combine thoroughly.

If desired, top with seasoned bread crumbs and additional parmesan cheese.

Place in the oven for 30 minutes, or until golden.

Sausage Potato Hash in the Morning

4-6 people

Time to prepare: 10 minutes

Time to cook: 20 minutes

Ingredients: 1 pound pork breakfast sausage, crumbled

12 cups yellow onion, diced cups potatoes, shredded and patted dry

1 tsp. garlic powder

12 teaspoons fresh thyme

1 teaspoon sea salt

1 teaspoon ground black pepper

6 eggs

1 cup shredded mild cheddar cheese, and sliced
Scallions for garnish

Preheat the oven to broil.
Heat a 12-inch cast iron skillet over medium heat and
add the breakfast sausage. Brown for about 5 minutes
on medium heat. Remove the fat.
Combine the shredded potatoes and onion in a mixing
bowl. Combine with cooked sausage. Garlic powder,
thyme, salt, and black pepper to taste.
Firmly press the sausage and potato mixture into the
bottom of the pan with the back of a wooden spoon to
form a firm layer. Cook for 3-5 minutes, stirring
occasionally, on medium-high heat.
Gently lift the crust to check for brownness and
crispness. Once the potatoes have developed a nice
crispy texture, gently flip them over and cook for
another 3 minutes.
Over the potato and sausage crust, crack the eggs and
top with shredded mild cheddar cheese.
Remove the skillet from the heat and place it under the
broiler for 5-7 minutes, or until the eggs are done to
your liking.
Before serving, garnish with fresh scallions.

Pie with Chorizo

4-6 people
Time to prepare: 15 minutes
Time to cook: 30 minutes

1 pound chorizo sausage, crumbled 1 cup red onion,
diced 4 garlic cloves, crushed and minced 12 cup
poblano pepper, diced 12 cups red bell pepper, diced
tablespoon ancho chili powder
a teaspoon of cumin
1 teaspoon cilantro
14 cups chopped fresh cilantro
1 12 cup fresh kernels
1 15-ounce can drain kidney beans 1 28-ounce can be
crushed tomatoes

1 cup chicken or vegetable stock 12 cup queso cheese, crumbled; 12 cup cheddar cheese, shredded; 12 cups melted butter

1 pound cornmeal

a cup of flour a teaspoon of baking powder

2 beaten eggs, 1 tablespoon orange juice

a tablespoon of honey

14 cups of buttermilk

1 quart sour cream

12 teaspoons of salt

Preheat oven to 425°F/218°C before beginning.

Heat the chorizo in a 12-inch cast iron skillet over medium heat. 5 minutes in the oven

Combine the onion, garlic, poblano pepper, and red bell pepper in a mixing bowl. Cook for 4-5 minutes, stirring frequently. Season with ancho chili powder, cumin, coriander, and cilantro, to taste. Stir thoroughly.

Combine the corn kernels, kidney beans, tomatoes, liquid, and vegetable or chicken stock in a mixing bowl. Bring to a boil by increasing the heat to medium-high. Remove from the heat and stir in the queso and cheddar cheeses.

Combine the cornmeal, flour, and baking powder in a mixing bowl. Add the butter, eggs, orange juice, honey, buttermilk, sour cream, and salt one at a time. Mix until well combined.

Spread the cornmeal mixture evenly over the top of the skillet.

Bake the skillet for 20 minutes, or until the cornmeal crust is golden brown and firm.

Apple Cider Baked Pork

6 people
Time to prepare: 10 minutes
Time to cook: 45 minutes

2 to 3 pounds of pork tenderloin roast 14 cup olive oil (distributed)
1 cup sliced sweet yellow onions 3 crushed and minced garlic cloves

1 teaspoon red pepper flakes, crushed
1 paprika teaspoon
1 teaspoon fresh thyme
1-quart apple cider
3 cups red baking apples, peeled and cut into wedges
12 teaspoon nutmeg 3 cups cubed sweet potatoes
12 teaspoon cilantro 1 teaspoon sea salt
1 teaspoon ground black pepper

Preheat oven to 425°F/218°C before beginning.
Make a 12-inch cast iron skillet with 2 tablespoons of olive oil. Heat over medium heat.
Mix in the onion and garlic. Cook for 2-3 minutes.
The tenderloin should be seasoned with crushed red pepper flakes, paprika, and thyme. Brown the tenderloin evenly on all sides in the skillet, about 2-3 minutes per side. Pour in the apple cider and bring to a simmer.
Meanwhile, in a mixing bowl, combine the baked apples and sweet potatoes. Season with nutmeg, coriander, salt, and black pepper, and drizzle with the remaining olive oil. To coat, toss everything together. Combine the vegetables with the pork in the skillet. Place the skillet in the oven after it has been removed from the heat. Bake for 30-35 minutes, or until an internal temperature of 160°F/71°C is reached.
Allow 10 minutes to rest before serving.

Vegetables and large ranch chops

4 people
Time to prepare: 10 minutes
Time to cook: 35 minutes

4 bone-in pork chops, about 8 ounces each, 34 to 1-inch
thick
2 tbsp of olive oil
4 cups halved small red potatoes
4 cups washed and trimmed green beans
1 tablespoon fresh dill, chopped 12 cups fresh parsley,
chopped 4 crushed and minced garlic cloves
1 paprika teaspoon
1 teaspoon black pepper 1 teaspoon salt

Preheat the oven to 400 degrees Fahrenheit/204 degrees
Celsius.
Brush olive oil into a 12-inch cast iron skillet. In the
pan, place the pork chops.
Combine the potatoes and green beans in a mixing
bowl. Toss with the remaining olive oil to coat.
Combine the vegetables with the pork chops in the pan.
Dill, parsley, garlic, paprika, salt, and black pepper to
taste. Bake the skillet for 30-35 minutes, or until the
potatoes are tender and the pork chops are cooked
through.

Spaghetti with Italian Sausage Baked

4 people
Time to prepare: 10 minutes
Time to cook: 30 minutes

1 pound ground Italian sausage (ground)
1 tbsp. vegetable oil
4 crushed and minced garlic cloves
1 cup diced yellow onion
1 can crushed tomatoes (28 oz.) with liquid
14 cups chopped fresh parsley 12 cups chopped fresh
basil 1 tablespoon fresh oregano 1 teaspoon salt
teaspoon black pepper cups chicken stock or water
12lb spaghetti noodles
12 cups pearled fresh mozzarella
12 cup freshly grated parmesan cheese

Preheat oven to 400°F/204°C before beginning.

Heat the vegetable oil in a 12-inch cast iron skillet over medium-high heat. Cook the Italian sausage in the pan until it is browned, about 5-7 minutes. Excess grease should be drained from the skillet.

Combine the garlic and yellow onion in a mixing bowl. Cook for another 2-3 minutes, or until the onions are tender.

Season with parsley, basil, oregano, salt, and black pepper and add the tomatoes and liquid. Stir thoroughly. Bring the chicken stock or water to a low boil. Push the pasta into the pan to ensure that the sauce covers the noodles. Cook, stirring occasionally, for 10-12 minutes, or until the pasta is al dente.

Combine the mozzarella and parmesan cheeses in a mixing bowl. Bake the skillet in the oven for 15-20 minutes.

Medallions of Cinnamon-Scented Pork

4 people
Time to prepare: 10 minutes
Time to cook: 25 minutes

1 pound pork tenderloin, cut into 1-inch-thick medallions
12 tsp coarse sea salt
1 teaspoon black pepper, cracked
1 tbsp. vegetable oil
3 cups asparagus spears (1-inch pieces)

2 tbsp. melted butter
1 stick cinnamon
12 cups dry white wine 3 cups sliced portabella or wild
mushrooms
12 cup chicken broth 12 teaspoons ground nutmeg 1
teaspoon fresh thyme
1 teaspoon cornstarch
1 tbsp. ice cold water

Preparation: Heat the olive oil in a 12-inch deep cast
iron skillet over medium-high heat.
Season the pork medallions with black pepper and salt.
Cook the pork in the pan until browned, about 4-5
minutes per side.
Sauté the asparagus for 2-3 minutes, or until the color
brightens.
Transfer the pork medallions and asparagus to a plate to
serve.
Melt the butter and add the cinnamon stick over
medium heat. Cook for 1-2 minutes, or until the mixture
is fragrant.
Before adding the white wine, sauté the mushrooms for
2 minutes. Reduce the heat for 2-3 minutes.
Combine the chicken stock, nutmeg, and thyme in a
mixing bowl. Allow cooking while you make a smooth
paste with the cornstarch and water.
To the sauce, add the cornstarch mixture. Cook, stirring
constantly until the sauce thickens slightly.

Before serving, drizzle the sauce over the pork and asparagus.

Casserole with Sweet Peas and Pork

4 people
Time to prepare: 10 minutes
Time to cook: 15 minutes

1 pound ground pork tablespoon olive oil garlic cloves crushed and minced cup carrots, diced12 cup celery, diced cups fresh sweet peas

2 teaspoons grated fresh ginger

2 teaspoons chopped fresh lemongrass

2 tbsp of soy sauce

1 teaspoon oyster sauce

1 tablespoon vinegar (rice)

4 cups cooked jasmine rice

1 teaspoon black pepper 1 teaspoon salt

For garnish, use chopped fresh scallions.

Preparation: Heat the oil in a 10- or 12-inch cast iron skillet over medium heat. Combine the garlic, carrots, and celery in a mixing bowl. Cook for 3-4 minutes, stirring constantly.
Cook for 5 minutes, or until the pork is browned.
Season with ginger, lemongrass, soy sauce, oyster sauce, and rice vinegar before adding the peas. Combine thoroughly.
Season the rice with salt and black pepper. Continue to heat for 3-4 minutes more.
Garnish with fresh scallions before serving.

Whitefish with Spicy Lemon Sauce

4 people

Time to prepare: 10 minutes

Time to cook: 15 minutes

1 pound whitefish fillets 14 cup butter teaspoon smoked paprika
12 teaspoon cayenne pepper, crushed red pepper flakes
2 crushed and minced garlic cloves
1 teaspoon sea salt
1 tsp black pepper 1 cup vegetable or chicken stock 2 tbsp lemon juice
4 cups dark leafy greens like chard
2 tbsp. lemon zest
Garnish with fresh lemon wedges
Serving Cayenne pepper sauce

Prepare the paprika, cayenne powder, crushed red pepper, garlic, salt, and black pepper in a mixing bowl. Season the whitefish fillets on both sides with the spice mixture.
Melt the butter in a 12-inch cast iron skillet over medium heat. Cook for 3 minutes on each side after adding the fish to the pan.
Pour in the vegetable or chicken stock and lemon juice. Combine the dark, leafy greens and lemon zest in a mixing bowl. Toss gently. Cook for another 4-5 minutes over medium heat, or until the greens are tender.
Garnish with fresh lemons and serve with cayenne pepper sauce on the greens for extra spice.

Salmon braised in white wine with baked potatoes

4 people
Time to prepare: 10 minutes
Time to cook: 25 minutes

Ingredients:
1 pound salmon fillets tbsp olive oil cloves crushed and
minced garlic
1 tbsp. fresh dill, 1 tbsp. fresh chives
12 cups dry white wine 1 teaspoon lemon zest
cups washed and trimmed green beans thinly sliced
yellow potatoes
2 tsp. fresh rosemary
1 teaspoon black pepper 1 teaspoon salt

Preheat oven to 425°F/218°C before beginning.

Warm the olive oil in a 10-inch cast iron skillet over medium heat. Sauté the garlic for 1 minute.

Season the salmon with dill, chives, and lemon zest.

Cook for two minutes after adding the white wine to the skillet.

To the pan, add the green beans. Then, evenly layer the potato slices over the salmon and green beans. Season the potatoes with rosemary, salt, and freshly ground black pepper.

Bake the skillet for 15-20 minutes, or until the salmon is flaky and pink.

Piccata de Shrimp

4 people
Time to prepare: 10 minutes
Time to cook: 15 minutes

1 pound raw shrimp, cleaned and deveined tablespoons
butter cloves crushed and minced garlic

14 cups sliced shallots
14 cups capers
14 cups fresh lemon juice
1 cup white wine, dry
12 cup chicken broth
1 teaspoon sea salt
1 teaspoon ground black pepper
12 lb angel hair pasta
Garnish with fresh parsley

Preparation: Melt the butter in a 10- or 12-inch cast iron skillet over medium heat.
Stir in the garlic and shallots. Cook for about 1-2 minutes.
Cook the shrimp for 2 minutes, gently tossing them.
In the skillet, combine the capers, lemon juice, and white wine. Allow the wine to reduce for about 1-2 minutes.
Combine the chicken stock, salt, and black pepper in a mixing bowl. Stir thoroughly. Bring to a low boil by increasing the heat to medium-high.
Reduce the heat to medium and cook the angel hair pasta for 7-10 minutes, or until the pasta is al dente.
Garnish with fresh parsley and serve.

Paella with shrimp and chorizo

4-6 people
Time to prepare: 10 minutes
Time to cook: 40 minutes

14 cups extra virgin olive oil
1 cup diced red onion
1 cup diced green bell pepper 4 crushed and minced
garlic cloves
1 pound crumbled chorizo sausage 14 cup tomato paste
smoked paprika 1 teaspoon
12 teaspoon cayenne pepper powder
1 cup white wine, dry
1 cup chicken broth
3 cups rice, cooked

12 pounds cleaned and deveined raw shrimp

Preheat the oven to 425°F/218°C before beginning.
Warm the olive oil in a 10- or 12-inch cast iron skillet over medium heat.
Cook for 5 minutes, or until the chorizo is browned. Remove any excess grease.
Combine the red onion, green bell pepper, and garlic in a mixing bowl. Sauté until the onions and peppers start to soften, about 4 minutes.
Season with tomato paste, smoked paprika, and cayenne pepper powder to taste. Stir thoroughly.
Allow the white wine to reduce for 5 minutes. Combine the chicken stock and cooked rice in a mixing bowl. Stir thoroughly.
Bake the skillet in the oven for 20 minutes. Remove the shrimp and replace them.
Return the skillet to the oven and bake for another 10 minutes, or until the shrimp are cooked through.

Scallops with Sweet and Spicy Sauce

4 people
Time to prepare: 10 minutes
Time to cook: 15 minutes

Ingredients:
2 tbsp. olive oil
6 cups chopped bok choy
2 tbsp. melted butter
20 to 16 sea scallops
4 crushed and minced garlic cloves
12 cup sugar 1 tablespoon jalapeno pepper, diced
14 cups of rice vinegar
12 cups of water
1 teaspoon sea salt
1 teaspoon ground black pepper

Preparation: Heat the olive oil in a 10 or 12-inch cast
iron skillet over medium heat. Cook until the bok choy
is crisp-tender, about 4-5 minutes. Set aside after
removing from the pan. Stay warm.
Melt the butter in the skillet over medium heat.
Combine the scallops, garlic, and jalapeno pepper in a
mixing bowl. Cook the scallops for 1-2 minutes per side
while tossing the other ingredients lightly.
In the skillet, combine the sugar, rice vinegar, and
water. Cook for 3-4 minutes, stirring frequently, to
allow flavors to blend.

Serve the scallops with the sauce over sautéed bok choy.

Crab Chowder with Smoked Bacon

4-6 people
Time to prepare: 10 minutes
Time to cook: 30 minutes

Ingredients: 12 pound bacon, 1 cup sweet yellow onion, 1 cup celery, 1 cup carrots, diced

1 tablespoon thyme, fresh

1 teaspoon black pepper 1 teaspoon salt 12 cup white
wine, dry

8 cups cubed red potatoes 2 cups whole milk

2 cups fish broth

1 quart heavy cream

1 quart clam juice

1 pound of crabmeat

For garnish, use fresh scallions.

Preparation: Heat a 12-inch skillet over medium heat
and cook the bacon until lightly crisp, about 5 minutes.
Mix in the yellow onion, celery, and carrots. Thyme,
salt, and black pepper to taste. Cook for 3-4 minutes.
Cook for another 1-2 minutes after adding the white
wine.

Combine the potatoes, milk, fish stock, heavy cream,
and crab juice in a mixing bowl. Stir thoroughly.
Increase the heat to medium-high and cook, stirring
frequently, for 10 minutes, or until the potatoes are
tender.

Half of the mixture should be blended in a blender until
smooth. Reintroduce the blended mixture to the skillet.
Cook until the crab meat is heated through, about 7-10
minutes.

Garnish with scallions, if desired.

Alfredo with Cajun Shrimp

4 people
Time to prepare: 10 minutes
Time to cook: 20 minutes

Ingredients:
12 cups melted butter

14 cups sliced shallots
3 crushed and minced garlic cloves
14 cups white wine, dry
14 cup flour 1/4 cup chicken stock 1/4 cup heavy cream
two teaspoons Cajun flavoring
1 teaspoon sea salt
1 teaspoon ground black pepper
1 cup freshly grated parmesan cheese
1 pound cleaned and deveined shrimp
12 pounds of linguine noodles
Garnish with lemon wedges

Preparation: Melt butter in a 12-inch cast iron skillet over medium heat.
Stir in the garlic and shallots. Cook for 1-2 minutes.
Allow the white wine to reduce for 2 minutes before adding the flour. Using a spoon, combine the flour until it forms a smooth paste.
Stir constantly as you gradually add the chicken stock and heavy cream. Cajun seasoning, salt, and black pepper to taste. Incorporate the parmesan cheese.
Cook the pasta for 7-10 minutes, or until al dente, over medium heat.
Simmer the shrimp in the sauce for 2-3 minutes before adding the pasta.
Garnish with fresh lemon slices.

Skillet Sweet Potato Burrito

4 people
Time to prepare: 10 minutes
Time to cook: 30 minutes

2 12 cups sweet potatoes, cubed 14 cup olive oil,
divided 1 cup yellow onion, diced 3 garlic cloves,
crushed and minced cup red bell peppers, chopped cups
tomatoes, diced 1 cup rice
1 drained 15-ounce can black beans
1 12 cup fresh kernels
1 tsp. chili powder
1 tablespoon cumin
1 paprika teaspoon
1 teaspoon black pepper 1 teaspoon salt
14 cups chopped fresh cilantro 2 12 cup veggie broth
1 cup queso de Mexico
1 cup shredded cheddar cheese
Topping: sour cream

Prepare a 10- or 12-inch cast iron skillet by heating 2
tablespoons olive oil over medium heat. Cook for 7-8
minutes, stirring occasionally, with the sweet potatoes.
If necessary, add an additional 2 tablespoons olive oil
along with the onion, garlic, and red bell pepper. Cook
for another 5 minutes.

Combine the tomatoes, rice, black beans, and corn kernels in a mixing bowl. Toss with chili powder, cumin, paprika, salt, black pepper, and cilantro to combine.

Increase the heat to high and add the vegetable broth. Reduce the heat to low and cover for 15 minutes, or until the rice is tender.

Allow the queso and Mexican cheeses to melt before serving.

Serve with sour cream on top.

Pasta with Lemony Wild Mushrooms and Broccoli

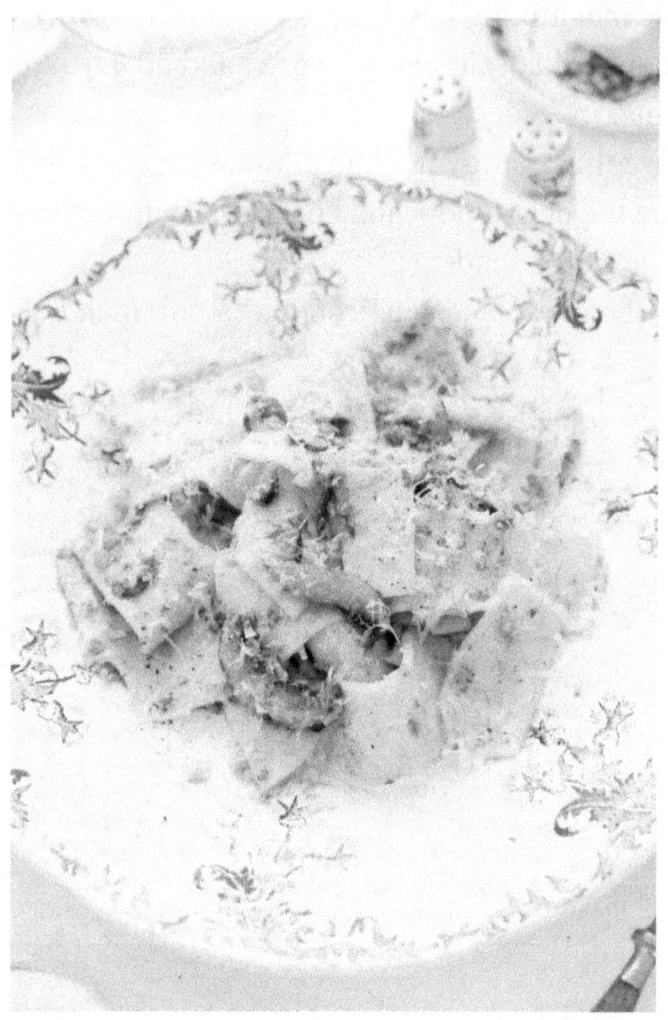

4 people
Time to prepare: 10 minutes
Time to cook: 15 minutes

Ingredients:
2 cups florets broccoli

2 tbsp olive oil, cloves divided cup vegetable stock or
water, crushed and minced garlic
1 pound linguine pasta
4 cups thinly sliced wild mushrooms
2 tbsp of lemon juice
teaspoon fresh thyme 1 tablespoon lemon zest
1 tablespoon chopped fresh chives
1 teaspoon sea salt
1 teaspoon ground black pepper
For garnish, use freshly grated asiago cheese.

Prepare the wild mushrooms with 1 tablespoon of olive
oil, lemon juice, lemon zest, thyme, chives, salt, and
black pepper in a mixing bowl. Toss to combine.
1 tablespoon olive oil, heated in a 10- or 12-inch cast
iron skillet over medium heat Sauté the broccoli florets
until they are bright green and slightly tender. Set aside
in the same bowl as the mushrooms.
Heat the vegetable stock or water in a skillet over
medium-high heat until it is lightly boiling. Cook for
about 7-10 minutes, or until the linguine noodles are al
dente. Remove any excess liquid.
Add the broccoli and mushroom mixture to the linguine
in the pan. Toss over medium-low heat until all
ingredients are warmed through and well combined.
Before serving, toss with fresh asiago cheese.

Pot Pie with Root Vegetables

4-6 people
Time to prepare: 15 minutes
Time to cook: 50 minutes

Ingredients: 2 tbsp olive oil
12 cup butter 14 cups + 1 tablespoon flour 1 cup yellow
onion, sliced 3 cloves garlic, crushed and minced 1 cup
red potatoes, cubed 1 cup carrots, sliced 1 cup sweet
potato, cubed 1 cup beets, cubed
12 cup vegetable broth
1-quart heavy cream
1 teaspoon fresh tarragon
12 tsp celery seed
1 teaspoon dried oregano

1 tsp salt 1 tsp black pepper refrigerated pie crust doughs

Preheat oven to 425°F/218°C before beginning.

Lay out one of the pie crust doughs flat. Cut out as many pieces of dough as possible with a small cookie cutter, approximately 1-2 inches in any shape, and set aside. These will be used to make a decorative edging for the skillet's crust gap.

Heat the olive oil in a 10-inch skillet over medium heat. Combine the onions and garlic in a mixing bowl. Cook until the vegetables are tender, about 2-3 minutes.

Combine the red potatoes, carrots, sweet potatoes, and beets in a mixing bowl. Cook, stirring occasionally, for 7 minutes, or until the vegetables begin to tenderize. Set aside after removing from the pan.

Cook until the butter is melted in the pan. Stir in the flour constantly until a browned paste forms. Slowly pour in the vegetable stock and heavy cream, whisking constantly to incorporate the flour mixture and create a thick sauce.

Tarragon, celery seed, oregano, salt, and black pepper to taste. Stir in the vegetables once more. Remove the pan from the heat and set aside to cool slightly.

One pie crust should be placed in the center of the pan. Use the cut-out pieces to bridge the gap between the crust and the pan's rim all around the edge. Gently press to seal.

Bake for 30 to 35 minutes, or until the crust is golden brown.

Parmesan-Zesty Eggplant

4 people
Time to prepare: 10 minutes
Time to cook: 30 minutes

14 cups vegetable oil medium-sized eggplant, sliced roughly 14-inch thick eggs, beaten
1 cup bread crumbs, seasoned
1 garlic clove, crushed and minced cup freshly grated parmesan cheese, divided 12 cup marinara sauce prepared (homemade or jarred)
1 tbsp. fresh oregano

14 cups chopped fresh basil (additional for garnish, if desired)
1 teaspoon sea salt
1 teaspoon ground black pepper
1 cup sliced fresh mozzarella cheese 6 cups dark salad greens for serving

Preheat oven to 350°F/177°C before beginning.
In one bowl, combine the beaten eggs, and in another, combine the seasoned bread crumbs, garlic, and 12 cups of parmesan cheese.
Heat the vegetable oil in a 12-inch cast iron skillet over medium-high heat.
Dredge each eggplant slice through the breadcrumb mixture after coating it with the beaten egg.
Cook for 2 minutes per side, or until the eggplant slices are browned. As you work through the eggplant in batches, place cooked pieces on a side plate.
Turn off the heat and arrange all of the eggplant pieces in the bottom of the skillet. Season with oregano, basil, salt, and black pepper, and top with marinara sauce.
Top the eggplant with the remaining 12-cup parmesan cheese and mozzarella cheese.
Bake for 20 minutes, or until the cheese has turned golden brown.
Serve with dark, fresh salad greens.

Casserole of Italian Beans and Tomatoes

4-6 people
Time to prepare: 10 minutes

Time to cook: 35 minutes

14 cups vegetable oil, 3 cups day-old French bread,
cubed 6 cups heirloom tomatoes, chopped 1 cup sweet
yellow onion, diced 4 garlic cloves, crushed and minced
1 teaspoon honey
1 teaspoon sea salt
1 teaspoon ground black pepper
3 cups cooked cannellini beans
12 cups fresh basil, chopped 3 cups fresh spinach, torn
1 teaspoon crushed red pepper flakes 1 tablespoon
lemon zest
12 cup freshly grated parmesan cheese

Preheat oven to 350°F/177°C before beginning.
Warm the vegetable oil in a 12-inch cast iron skillet
over medium heat. Add the cubed bread to the pan and
toss for 5 minutes, or until the bread cubes are nicely
toasted.
Combine the tomatoes, onion, and garlic in a mixing
bowl. Honey, salt, and black pepper to taste. Cook,
stirring constantly, for 5 minutes, or until tomatoes
soften.
Combine the cannellini beans, spinach, basil, lemon
zest, and crushed red pepper flakes in a mixing bowl.
Toss to combine.
Drizzle olive oil and parmesan cheese over the
casserole. Bake for 20-25 minutes in a preheated oven.

Pasta with Creamy Green Vegetables in a Skillet

4 people
Time to prepare: 10 minutes
Time to cook: 15 minutes

14 cups unsalted butter
2 garlic cloves, crushed and minced 14 cups sliced
scallions 2 cups broccoli florets
2 cups sliced zucchini 2 cups torn spinach
12 teaspoons red pepper flakes, crushed
1 teaspoon sea salt
1 teaspoon ground black pepper
1 cup veggie stock
12 c. heavy cream
12 cups softened cream cheese

12 cup freshly grated parmesan cheese 14 cups fresh basil, chopped 12 cups fresh parsley, chopped 1 tablespoon fresh chives, chopped 1 pound bow tie pasta, cooked

If desired, garnish with lemon zest.

Preparation: Melt the butter in a 12-inch cast iron skillet over medium heat. Cook for 1 minute after adding the garlic and scallions.

Combine the broccoli and zucchini. Cook for 2-3 minutes. Add the spinach to the skillet and cook for another 1-2 minutes. Season with salt, black pepper, and crushed red pepper.

Set aside the vegetable mixture from the skillet.

Add the vegetable stock to the skillet and bring to a boil over medium-high heat. Turn the heat down to medium.

Slowly whisk in the heavy cream, followed by the cream cheese, until a smooth consistency is achieved.

Reduce to low heat and stir in the parmesan cheese, basil, parsley, and chives. Combine thoroughly.

Return the vegetables and pasta to the pan and toss to combine. Allow simmering for 3-4 minutes, or until thoroughly warmed.

If desired, garnish with lemon zest.

Chinese Noodles with Bok Choy

4 people
Time to prepare: 10 minutes
Time to cook: 15 minutes

14 cups roasted peanut oil
1 cup vegetable stock 1 pound baby bok choy, halved
lengthwise
14 cups natural creamy peanut butter
2 tbsp. soy sauce
2 teaspoons garlic chili paste
1 tsp honey 1 tbsp fresh grated ginger cloves crushed
and minced garlic
12 teaspoons red pepper flakes, crushed
12 oz. cooked Chinese flat noodles
Scallions, sliced for garnish 2 teaspoons sesame oil

Preparation: Heat the peanut oil in a 10-inch cast iron
skillet over medium heat. Cook the bok choy for 2
minutes on each side. Set aside after removing from the
pan.
Add the vegetable stock, peanut butter, and soy sauce to
the skillet. Cook over medium heat, stirring constantly,
until smooth.
Combine the chili garlic paste, honey, fresh ginger,
garlic, and crushed red pepper in a mixing bowl.
Combine thoroughly.
Toss the noodles into the skillet.

Arrange the bok choy on individual serving plates.
Drizzle sesame oil over equal portions of the noodles
and box Choy.
Before serving, garnish with scallions.

Linguine in Greece

4 people
Time to prepare: 10 minutes
Time to cook: 15 minutes

14 cups plus two tablespoons olive oil 4 cups chopped
tomatoes 4 crushed and minced garlic cloves
2 cups shredded spinach
1 teaspoon sea salt
1 teaspoon ground black pepper
1 teaspoon of lemon juice

12 cup canned artichoke hearts, drained 12 cup
Kalamata olives, sliced 1 pound cooked linguine
noodles
1 tbsp. fresh oregano
12 cups chopped fresh parsley 1 cup crumbled feta
cheese

Prepare a 10-inch cast iron skillet by heating 2
tablespoons olive oil over medium heat. Combine the
tomatoes and garlic in a mixing bowl. Sauté for 4-5
minutes, or until tomatoes begin to break down slightly.
Season the spinach with salt, black pepper, and lemon
juice. Cook for another 2 minutes.
Combine the artichoke hearts, Kalamata olives, and
linguine noodles in a mixing bowl. Toss to combine and
heat thoroughly.
Drizzle the remaining olive oil over the noodles as
desired. Add oregano, parsley, and feta cheese to taste.
Toss to combine.
Serve immediately while still hot.

Hash of Crisp Green Beans and Eggs

4-6 people
Time to prepare: 10 minutes
Time to cook: 25 minutes

Ingredients:
12 cups of water
2 cups washed and trimmed fresh green beans
2 tbsp of olive oil
6 cups diced red potatoes 3 garlic cloves crushed 1
green bell pepper diced 1 tablespoon fresh dill, chopped

1 tablespoon fresh chives, chopped 1 teaspoon salt 1
teaspoon black pepper
6 eggs

Preparation: Heat the water in a 12-inch cast iron skillet.
Heat the green beans over medium-high heat. Cook,
stirring in the water until the green is bright but still
crisp. Remove from the pan and drain any remaining
water.
Heat the olive oil in the pan over medium heat.
Combine the potatoes, garlic, and bell pepper in a
mixing bowl. Toss to combine.
Spread the mixture evenly in the pan, pressing slightly
down. Cook for about 15 minutes, flipping once, or
until potatoes are crisp on the outside.
Return the green beans to the pan and season with dill,
chives, salt, and black pepper to taste. Toss gently.
Each egg should be cracked individually over the
vegetable hash. Cook for another 5 minutes, or until the
egg whites are set and the yolks are done to your liking.

Chili with White Beans and Southern Greens

4-6 people
Time to prepare: 10 minutes
Time to cook: 30 minutes

1 tablespoon extra virgin olive oil
3 cloves garlic, crushed and minced 1 cup green bell
pepper, diced cup tomatillos, chopped cups collard
greens, chopped
1 tablespoon cumin
1 teaspoon of chili powder
1 lime juice tablespoon
14 cup chopped fresh cilantro cups cooked or canned
cannellini beans cups vegetable stock
12 cup chopped canned roasted green chilies

Preparation: Heat the olive oil in a 12-inch skillet over medium heat.

Combine the onion, garlic, and green bell pepper in a mixing bowl. Sauté for 4-5 minutes, or until slightly tender.

Cook for 3 minutes more, or until the tomatillos are softened.

Combine the collard greens, cumin, chili powder, lime juice, cilantro, and cannellini beans in a mixing bowl. Toss to combine.

Combine the vegetable stock and green chilies in a mixing bowl. Bring the chili to a low boil over medium-high heat. Reduce the heat to low, cover, and cook for 15 to 20 minutes.

12 cups of the chili should be blended until smooth. Stir the mixture back into the chili.

Serve right away.

Conclusion

Keep in mind that the purpose of this book is to demonstrate the versatility of cast iron skillet cooking, not to address dietary restrictions. While fresh ingredients are used whenever possible, if you find that any of these recipes are too high in caloric or fat content, each of these recipes will stand up beautifully to simple modifications. The point is that you realize how simple and delicious it can be to prepare meals in this time-honored method that will become household staples for years to come.

My hope is that you will embrace cast iron cooking for the benefits it offers. Those benefits include the ability to prepare fresh meals at home, the ability to save time by simplifying overcomplicated dishes and condensing the flavor into one delicious skillet, and the ability to use your imagination as you explore the many wonders of cast iron cooking on your own.